ROUTINE, FOCUS AND MENTAL FREEDOM

The Tools Are Here.

Have you dreamed of becoming a collegiate gymnast or an Olympian? Have you pushed through workouts only to come home discouraged and unfulfilled? Are you stuck on a plateau of unrealized dreams?

In this practical, easy to understand and action-oriented book, Amy Twiggs, Director of Flippin' Awesome Gymnastics, will help you solidify a productive athletic daily routine.

Twiggs has personally used every piece of information in this book herself for many years in her successful career.

> Twiggs explains "As a former competitive gymnast, I've been there-- I know what it feels like to try your best and to fail. I also know how it feels to work hard to achieve your goals. I know what it feels like to be overwhelmed in the daily tasks of athletic life, of wishing you could be more productive during practice, or searching for a desire to work hard when your goals repeatedly go unfulfilled."

Flippin' Awesome Gymnast, Vol. II reveals a proven approach designed to resolve your struggles with unproductive use of time and a loss of enjoyment in the gym. It unveils tools to keep your mind focused on your goals.

You may be asking yourself:
How is it possible to use my time any more efficiently? How can I actually create what I want to feel at workout before the day even starts? And how can I ever reach the goals I dream of accomplishing?

In this how-to guide, you'll be given tools to:

- Find purpose and excitement in each practice and competition
- Construct a personal daily routine for maximum athletic results
- Create a personal nutrition plan to increase energy and safety at gym
- Dramatically improve your ability to remain calm and decrease anxiety
- Increase consistency in your current gymnastics skills and routines

No matter your current ability, this book provides proven strategies to use your time more productively towards your athletic goals. It addresses the changes necessary to create your own personal **elite-level gymnastics day**.

Each day as a gymnast is a **GIFT**; embrace it!

Making no change to your daily gymnastics routine is like living your past presently. It's time to pass Level 1.   **3-2-1 Go!**

FLIPPIN' AWESOME GYMNAST

VOL. II

**5 Tools to Create Your
Elite-level Gymnastics
Day**

Amy Twiggs

ISBN-13: 978-1-949015-02-7

TABLE OF CONTENTS

Dedication

I would like to dedicate this book to the following people:

MY PARENTS

They have always been my greatest fans. Their dedication to my personal and athletic success continues to inspire me. I'm continually grateful for their guidance and unconditional love.

MY HUSBAND, TYLER

He has supported my efforts to strive to become someone better than I was yesterday. His patience and sacrifice on my behalf is endearing and appreciated.

FOUR WONDERFUL TEENAGERS

Every day, I get to learn from my teenagers. They are each unique. However, together, they make an entertaining and dynamic team. Much of my joy comes from being near these amazing youth.

Every gymnast, coach and team I have had the pleasure of working with, thank you!

AND ALL OF YOU WHO ARE READING THIS BOOK
-THANK YOU-

INTRODUCTION

In the sport of gymnastics, the amount of hours required to reach the top level can be daunting. Every day, a gymnast must find balance between the right amount of sleep, the ideal nutrition, the most effective workouts, and necessary physical recovery time.

A gymnast must also be successful at home, in school, and in their social life. How does a gymnast find time to add their most important daily routine--the mental routine? This is a crucial factor to a gymnast's athletic success. Yet, it's also one of the most neglected areas of their daily schedules.

This book answers your athletic mental, physical, and emotional problems in an easy to implement format. The *Flippin' Awesome Gymnast* has been created to solve your daily time-management problems, utilizing a simple method. This book is for gymnasts who suffer from "overwhelm" in the midst of high-performance success.

As a competitive gymnast for over 15 years, including elite-level and collegiate level at Stanford University, I learned, of necessity, the importance of athletic time management and productivity. Every small daily choice can become a habit that will increase or diminish your future success as a gymnast. Gymnasts and any others who struggle with finding balance in their athletic careers will experience great success by putting into effect the principles found in this concise and helpful book.

Sierra, a former gymnast and current high school tumbler at a local high school, says, "The best part of this book is it can be read quickly and the tools are immediately helpful."

I promise that if you implement the five simple tools found in this book, you will immediately see and feel a difference in your ability to accomplish great things in a short time. You'll find your purpose for gymnastics deepen, your mental game become stronger, and your emotions will become pre-decided.

Don't be the person who misses out on opportunities in your athletic life because you take too long to get all of your daily tasks completed. Be the person who others look to for inspiration.

Be the kind of person others look at and say, "I don't know how you do it all." Be the kind of person who makes decisions and takes action now.

The tools you are about to learn have been used by many athletes to accomplish positive and lasting results. All you have to do to be in control of your athletic routine is to keep reading and apply the principles that are contained in this book.

Each principle will provide for you a new insight as you aim to keep the moments of greatness from slipping away. Take control of your life now; choose to be more productive and enjoy the new gymnastics daily routine as it becomes your launch pad to significant change. 3-2-1 Go!

My Story:

"Don't be afraid if things seem difficult in the beginning. That's only the initial impression. The important thing is not to retreat; you have to master yourself."

—Olga Korbut, gold medal gymnast

"There's no situation that will ever have power over you if you know who you are. Knowing who you are will change what you want.

Knowing what you want will change what you believe. Knowing what you believe creates a future of limitless possibilities!"

—Amy Twiggs

My elite routine began to develop when I was in kindergarten. I started gymnastics at the age of eight. Whether I was at the gym or watching the Olympics, I found myself intently observing higher-level gymnasts perform tricks that looked exhilarating. I was constantly imagining myself doing those same skills. Gymnastics became a part of my soul. It was woven into the fabric of my life. There was no separating gymnastics from me.

Just like any enthusiastic young gymnast, you would find me doing handstands and practicing the next skill outside our home on the grass or on the metal bars at my elementary school after the last bell rang. I recall ripping off a large part of the skin on my palm in the process of learning skills on those metal bars. What was a little flesh wound in exchange for feeling the rhythm of a bar kip as I would pop my body up onto the bar?

(A bar kip is a movement on the uneven parallel bars in which you glide your body under the bar, extend fully, and then pull yourself to a resting position with your stomach on the bar.)

In 3rd grade, I recall an elderly teacher with red curly hair who saw me working aerials, a maneuver in which you perform a cartwheel with no hands touching the ground. I was using the edge of the sidewalk outside this teacher's classroom door to practice. Instead of telling me to stop, she encouraged me to keep trying. I executed my first true aerial in front of that teacher and received an applause to boot.

At that time in my gymnastics career, I knew nothing about the importance of nutrition, sleep, and mental toughness; I just knew that I enjoyed flipping.

By the age of 15, I had progressed considerably as a gymnast. The Junior Olympics, or J.O., gymnastics program starts at level 1, progresses to level 10, and ends at Elite as the highest level. Level 10 and Elite gymnasts compete at college or in the Olympics. Typically, a competitive gymnast begins at level 3 then works through each level until they qualify for Elite.

During my club gymnastics years, I trained with the Arizona Twisters. At that time, Arizona Twisters didn't compete at level 10. Instead, the gymnasts would try out for elite after level 9. This was a legal and common path for many higher-level gymnasts at that time. I had attended two Elite qualification meets with two teammates, both of whom had reached the qualifying score on their first try, but I had not. They still came to the other qualifying meets just for more experience.

I didn't know it at the time, but my parents had purchased a necklace for me with my name and the word "elite" engraved on it, which they planned to give to me after the first qualifying meet. When I did finally qualify for elite after the third meet, my parents presented me with the necklace and I inquired about it. My dad told me he and my mom both knew I would become an elite eventually; there was no question in their minds. They knew it just like I did.

Failing at my first two attempts didn't discourage me from working a little harder to make my routines just a little better in order to progress further in the sport. This is the nature of gymnastics.

I currently love the song, "Get Back Up Again" from the movie, Trolls. To me, this is the perfect theme song for a gymnast's life. Every day, we fall in practice over and over, but we learn from day one of gymnastics that you always get back up again. There's no holding a gymnast down for long. Lingering in self-pity on the ground doesn't serve any gymnast well.

Around this same age, I was taught positive affirmations and visualization techniques by my older brother during the summer he spent home from college. These tools, along with relaxation and breathing techniques, became a consistent part of my daily routine. I attribute much of my confidence and success as an elite gymnast to those four tools.

At the age of 16, I experienced a kind of out-of-body episode because I had practiced visualization in such detail every night before I fell asleep. At that time, I was preparing for a National Team qualifying competition that was to take place at the Delta Center in Salt Lake City, Utah.

For six months prior to that competition, I had daily visualized the eight routines I was to perform. One tumbling pass, in particular, had caused me some anxiety in practice, but no longer held any power over me due to the visualization technique. Upon landing that tumbling pass at the competition, I experienced dèjá vu in a way I had never before felt it. The details of my routines were all performed precisely as I had envisioned them to be.

Although I had never actually been in the Delta Center, the arena layout, equipment set up, and general audience were everything I had imagined in my mind they would be. For a brief moment, I wasn't sure if I was in my bed at home visualizing this pass or actually performing at the arena.

Instantly, I knew there was power in the thoughts I had created in my mind and the words I had chosen to believe. It was beyond my ability to clearly explain. Since that experience at the Delta Center, I have used those same tools to adapt and refine my daily routine to become the person I am today.

I obtained a full-ride women's gymnastics scholarship and received a Psychology Degree from Stanford University. I am now a wife to an amazing man and a mother of four teenagers. I also own a gymnastics company, Flippin' Awesome Gymnastics, where I love to continually serve gymnasts.

My daily routine from the age of 15 to the present and in the future will continue to progress as I learn, understand, and gain more knowledge and life experience.

High-performing athletes often hear comments such as, "I don't know how you do all you do" or "Why do you want to do all that?" or "You should just sit and relax more often" or "I could never do what you do." Some call me "driven," "high energy," "non-stop," "exhausting to be around," and "crazy." Many people are astonished by the intense regimens that elite athletes choose.

Anyone can live an elite lifestyle if they choose to. Motive and desire are keys to any change. If you're reading this book, then chances are you have a desire to make changes to your current athletic routine.

I am offering athletic techniques that are applicable to everyone. If utilized, these tools will get you to a more impactful level of daily performance. This book will inspire greatness, increase confidence, and crush fears.

When you create your moments, days, dreams, and life, you're living intentionally. Do those hard things, make those uncomfortable choices, surprise yourself by exposing your own undiscovered capabilities. Elite performers narrow their daily choices to produce unimaginable results.

1

No Cruise Control

"I don't call them sacrifices. I call them exchanges."

—Shawn Johnson

"I'd rather regret the risks that didn't work out than the chances I didn't take at all."

—Simone Biles

CHAPTER 1 TOOLS:

No Cruise Control

A gymnast plans every day intentionally. You don't allow anyone to tell you what you can or cannot become. You are accountable to your inner voice. You live your gymnastics career to the highest level you can personally achieve.

The Range

This principle confirms the personal boundaries you, as a gymnast, create for yourself, the self-imposed limits within which you choose to live your life. These include the things that you're willing to sacrifice to become a high-performing gymnast.

When creating an elite-level daily routine, you need to understand that anything worth pursuing will require great sacrifices. Elite is the highest level of gymnastics for a reason. Each elite spent thousands of hours perfecting every mind and muscle command in order to achieve the designation of that level.

My husband, Tyler, and I recently were in the market for a new car. We did our research and found a car that had everything we thought we wanted or needed. Upon further inspection, we found out that it didn't come with cruise control. No cruise control? What 2017 car doesn't have cruise control? Who would choose to buy a car without cruise control?

Well, we did. It had everything else we were looking for. My sister, who never uses cruise control, claims that driving without cruise control keeps her more alert on the road. My sister was right, and that's how the name of this chapter was discovered, "No Cruise Control."

As I drove, I found my new car's speedometer pointed to a range between 50 mph and 90 mph. Initially, I wanted to be annoyed with the car.

I tried to convince myself, "The car should have had cruise control."

I ran through the same argument that I went through on the way to buy the car. Choosing to see it differently, I found my mind reflecting on my life. I don't like to be on autopilot or live my life without intention.

I deliberately choose my actions from 5:00 a.m. to 10:00 p.m. Just like my new car, I find that if I don't pay attention to a certain range of allowances in my life, I'll either get in trouble for speeding or I'll have to stop before I get to my intended destination.

I don't want either of those results. I want to reach my destination in the most efficient manner, at the most efficient speed, and with the least resistance. I want the life I live to always be intentional, mindful, and productive. As I drove my new car, I noticed that the more attentive I became to my surroundings with a watchful eye on my speedometer, the higher my car's fuel economy rate would go.

My husband took the car on a drive to Arizona a few weeks later and received a ticket for going 97 mph. That was unintentional, according to my husband. Being stopped for a ticket lengthens the travel time and makes the trip more expensive.

Upon hearing about this situation, I had even more respect for the car. It was clear that the quicker my husband wanted to get to his destination, the more valuable it would have been for him to decide upon the most efficient range to get there. In other words, neither selecting to drive 10 mph nor 160 mph will get you to your goals as efficiently as staying consistently within a moderate, safe, and legal range.

That range may be between 50-90 mph for you on your own trip to your destination. The tighter the range of choices I make, the more meaningful life is to me. I try to live life with no Cruise Control, and it works perfectly for me.

The range is defined as the boundaries you create for yourself. It comprises the self-imposed limits within which you choose to live your life. There are numerous choices and paths you can take every day.

Keeping a range between where you will and won't go or what you will and won't do, in the end, gives you a specific result, whether you want that result or not. Ralph Waldo Emerson states, *"That which we persist in doing becomes easier for us to do. Not that the nature of the thing is changed, but that our power to do is increased."* This is the range.

When you're not on cruise control, you won't allow yourself to go beyond a designated range, to either extreme, without understanding the consequences of doing so. Human nature is to avoid discomfort and seek pleasure.

Fear keeps us from progression. Fear may never leave. A desire for inaction may never leave. However, if you replace your fears and ineffective thoughts with a firm routine that keeps them in check, then they're always kept within a manageable range. You'll live a life that you have power over and can control.

How do we come up with a routine that constantly checks our thoughts? That question is the foundational basis of this book. By nature, we're pre-wired to want to stay within a certain limit. But it's important for us to recognize that if we want greater results than our natural minds create for us, we must be willing to give up some of life's comforts to get those results.

Nothing great ever comes without hard work and discomfort. If a speedometer gives a person an option to drive a car between zero and 160 mph, what range on that speedometer would you chose to stay between? If you don't go faster than 90 on the open highway, some may say you're ridiculous for not enjoying the maximum capabilities of your car. Some may say you drive way too fast.

No one can tell you what your range should be. The law mandates a range, but *you* get to choose if you'll obey the law. When you choose your own range, you're also choosing the consequences of that range. People will have opinions and try to influence your range, your risk, your enjoyment, your safety, and/or your satisfaction. But it all comes down to your choice of what you want and how you'll choose to get it.

What will you accept and what will you not accept in your life? Many people mock a person's choice of their life's range. This holds true for every area of your life. Anything worth doing will require you to let go of something you thought you could never let go of.

An elite athlete's range becomes narrower and more refined as they reach closer to their incomprehensible results. A life that most people look at as unbelievable, and only a few "crazy" people ever achieve, becomes reality for anyone willing to take small steps toward big results.

Growing up, I knew I could work out better when I made little changes to my food, sleep, daily routines, and work ethic. Whenever I had coaches or teammates tell me about a choice they made that helped them reach a goal, I would try to see if their proposition worked for me as well.

Many times during my life, I've heard comments such as, "How do you do what you do?" or "Why do you go to bed so early?" or "Why won't you eat this with us?" My favorite comment to hear was, "I could never do that." My immediate thought was, *Of course you could! You just need a reason.*

Nothing is too hard if your reason is from a place of love coming from within yourself. I chose to lose weight after my four children were born, because my knees hurt a lot and a doctor suggested I lose weight to ease the ache. The pain was my motivation. I found that if I lost weight, the pain left, but if I gained the weight back, the pain returned. I lost the weight and decided I liked the pain-free life, as well as some of the other benefits that came from the low weight.

My motivation changed to a personal love for myself and a life of service instead of pain. I now keep my weight range narrow, since it provides a result that feels good to me. I keep a daily routine that, to some observers, may seem strict, boring, and crazy, but provides much fulfillment to me for my life.

Chapter 1 Highlights

- Living a gymnast's life with No Cruise Control means you intentionally create your moments, days, dreams, and results.

- Turn off your Cruise Control and be an intentional gymnast.

- When you do those hard things and make those uncomfortable choices, you will surprise even yourself by exposing your own undiscovered capabilities.

- The Range is the self-imposed limits or boundaries you choose to live your life within.

- Elite performers must narrow their daily choices or range, which ultimately provides them with unimaginable and sometimes unexpected results.

What's ahead in Chapter 2

Find out how to start each day creating emotions of fulfillment as a gymnast and pre-planning every workout to be successful. Then, discover what you can do daily to show your gratitude to those who help you on your road to athletic accomplishment.

Chapter 1 Action Items

Journal:

1. What do you want?
2. What are the obstacles in your way?
3. To change your perspective, replace the word *Obstacle* (synonyms: trials, inconveniences, problems, difficulties) with *Opportunity* (synonyms: possibilities, to-do lists, blessings).
4. What are you specifically willing to do to get there?

2

The GIFT

"The best way to make your dreams come true is to wake up."

—Paul Valery

"Journal writing is a voyage to the interior."

—Christina Baldwin

"Once you make a decision, the universe conspires to make it happen."

—Ralph Waldo Emerson

CHAPTER 2 TOOLS:

GIFT is an acronym used to ignite and fan the flame of fire in your athletic soul every morning. It's your early morning journal-writing routine:

G = Gratitude, write one to five things you're grateful for about being a gymnast.

I = Inspiration, while reading, "free-write" your thoughts about gymnastics.

F = Feeling, write the answers to the questions: "How do I want to feel today?" "What will I do to make that happen?"

T = Thoughtfulness, write down one or two names of people you will serve today at gym.

My elite routine really began to develop when I was in kindergarten. I must have been told that keeping a journal was important, so I did. I didn't know what to write about at first, so I would sneak into my older sister's journal and copy her thoughts into my own. It was great.

From that point to the present, I've been a fairly consistent journal writer. Once I started gymnastics at the age of 8, I wrote about the skills I was working on, how I felt about being at gym, the coaches, the fears, the injuries, the successes, the teammates.

For many years, my journals consisted predominantly of athletic development. As I progressed athletically, I felt a constant need to ask for safety and help from God at every practice. My spiritual needs were recorded.

I constantly sought for inspiration from a higher power to help me become a better athlete. These conversations were recorded in my journal as well. Eventually, I realized the importance of giving back and incorporated in my writing ways to help others develop in the sport of gymnastics.

Initially, my journal consisted of cheap notebooks. In college, it was the Franklin Planner, which included my journal as well as every other schedule or goal toward which I was working. Now, my journaling habits have developed into a much more meaningful pattern that lifts me up at the beginning of every day and refocuses me at the end of the day.

My routine now is what I call my GIFT to myself during my morning journal writing and reading time. At night, I use the 10-year journal with only four-lines, which allows for a quick recap of my day. Even though I no longer compete, because I'm still a gymnast, I usually sit in my splits while I read and write in the mornings. Again, I choose my Range and live my life with No Cruise Control as much as possible.

I do a "free-write," which is something I learned from my freshman English teacher at Stanford. He would give us the assignment at the beginning of every class to write for five minutes without stopping or thinking. You hand-write your thoughts before your mind chooses to "think" your thoughts.

This is how I usually try to write in my morning routine. I consider my morning GIFT, a gift from God to me and from me to others.

Morning GIFT Routine

First, write the word GIFT in your journal every morning as a reminder that you get the gift to do gymnastics for another day. I keep my journal open during the GIFT routine, in case thoughts come throughout the process. Normally, I allow 15-30 minutes to work through the GIFT.

Next to each letter, write the following:

G = Gratitude

Begin every morning by writing one to five things you're grateful for about being a gymnast. Don't overthink; just write. Even on the hardest days, when you feel like giving up, you can find something for which to be grateful.

I = Inspiration

Next, continue to keep your journal open while you review your daily affirmations and goals. Read 10-20 minutes of inspiring and motivational texts. Write any inspirational, guided, or peaceful thoughts you want and receive during your reading time.

You might feel impressed to try something a little different on a skill or movement that has been causing you difficulty. You might enjoy an added measure of drive to overcome fear or develop patience during an especially long plateau of seemingly slow progress.

F = Feeling

You decide this one daily and it may be similar most days. You choose how you want to feel. No one has power to select your feelings for you, unless you give them that power. You must know what you want in order to be able to decide this clearly every day.

Ask yourself and answer these two questions in your journal:

1. How do I want to feel today? (e.g., energetic and courageous at gym)
2. How will I create that feeling? What will I do to make that happen?
   a. Write ideas such as:
      Enjoy a green shake for my morning protein because I know my body well enough that when I choose more greens/veggies, I have more energy to flip.
   b. I will do my daily affirmations as if they have already happened. I get to decide who I am today.
   c. I will do nighttime visualization to prepare for tomorrow's workout.
   d. I will do quick breathing techniques when I feel nervous or frustrated at gymnastics today.
   e. I will take a 20-minute power nap to give my body some recuperation time before practice.

T= Thoughtfulness

This is where you free-write and don't think too much. By now, you've opened your mind to inspiration through gratitude and inspirational texts. Trust your first instincts on one or two names of people.

Ask yourself: Whom can I serve today? This isn't a huge act of service. Choose something simple, such as cheering on a teammate, holding the door for a coach, encouraging a gymnast from a lower level, or smiling as you perform your routines. The benefits of giving back are undeniable and often unexpected.

This is one part of my life that took me years to discover and define. When you open your mind to look outside yourself, you create fulfillment and peace. Even when your days are tough in the gym, serving someone around you will ease that weight of personal frustration.

Just listen to what you feel in your heart and write a couple of names down. You could serve so many people every day. The effect of service is beyond your comprehension. Looking outside your needs changes you; it changes your neurological pathways, increases your sense of belonging and joy, and creates an awareness of others' needs.

Night Journal Routine

At night, I use a 10-year journal, sold by Because Time Flies, Inc., which includes only four lines. I love it. I can look back last year on each day and see what happened. I do more reflection on what actually happened each day in this journal.

Again, it takes me only a few minutes to record some of the day's highlights. It's worth the effort required to have these lasting memories. This is a great opportunity to see growth quickly. Sometimes, you may feel stuck, as if you haven't learned anything new in a very long time. The ability to look back over a couple of years quickly will be encouraging and remind you of all you've learned and accomplished in the gym.

Journaling is a catalyst for events that you want in your life. Your dreams aren't manifest without some intention. You must verbalize, write, and review them in order to help those dreams become a part of your life. This puts those ideas at the top of your mind and they become a part of who you are.

They are woven into your soul as you do your part to bring yourself closer to making those ideas become your reality. You don't just hope they happen; you make them happen by the little daily decisions that you choose.

Chapter 2 Highlights

- Writing down your thoughts, fears, dreams, and desires is like making a promise to your future self.

- What you write can be remembered; what you remember can be a learning tool.

- Journaling will keep you from repeating past mistakes and show you the progress you have made in your efforts to become an elite gymnast and person.

- GIFT stands for **G**ratitude, **I**nspiration, **F**eeling, **T**houghtfulness.

- GIFT is the morning journal routine to crush your fears and inspire confidence that will last your entire day.

- Lastly, end your day writing a quick review in a separate journal for personal accountability of your goals versus your actual performance that day.

- Journaling keeps you on track towards your dreams.

What's ahead in Chapter 3

You will learn the most simplified, yet powerful nutrition plan for your gymnastics performance every day. This food plan will help you feel and ready to excel toward becoming the best gymnast you are able to become.

Chapter 2 Action Items

Challenge:

1. Purchase two notebooks. Use one for your morning GIFT routine and one for your evening review journal time. Personalize this time for your needs.
2. Try the morning GIFT sequence for a month. Log any changes you feel or experiences in your practices and performances as a gymnast.
3. Review your workouts in a night journal. Think about what you might want to change for the next day to improve a skill or change a feeling while you're working out.

3

LIGHT

"A healthy outside starts from the inside."

— Robert Urich

"To eat is a necessity, but to eat intelligently is an art."

— La Rochefoucald

CHAPTER 3 TOOLS:

The Light Plan

The only food and nutrition plan that's personalized to fit every individual athlete perfectly. It's not only a physical food plan but also the mental and emotional plan in which the only question you must answer is: "Do I feel Light?"

Light foods: Any foods naturally made from the sunlight, which include fruit, veggies, grains, nuts, legumes, dairy, and meat.

Athletes are taught to eat food for fuel. It's imperative that athletes be wise about their food selection if they want to perform their best. What if we changed that a bit and decided to eat food for light?

I found that when I was competing as an elite gymnast for Arizona Twisters, I ate much more selectively than when I went to college. The college cafeterias provided selections of food to which I wasn't accustomed. In club gymnastics, the daily choices were spaghetti, legumes, eggs, oatmeal, and lots of grapefruit, which grew on our trees at home.

Not many more food options were usually available at home, so choices were consistent and easy. Food choices were simple not because we were a health-conscious family, but rather because we usually only had the basics. I didn't really need a nutritionist to help with my meal planning growing up.

In fact, I don't recall working with a regular nutritionist until I got to college. Growing up, I had an unknown tendency towards anemia. Roe Kreutzer, Arizona Twisters gymnastics owner, would request that my parents take me out for steak when she noticed that my energy was low. I just recall thinking this was a terrible idea, as I couldn't stand the feel, look, or taste of meat when I was growing up. I would plug my nose and swallow without chewing.

However, I didn't hesitate, as I only wanted the benefits that Roe's advice seemed to promise. Roe's observations and advice always worked. I did feel better at workouts. My energy had increased.

If anything could improve my athletics, I was all in. Bad taste or extra hard work didn't deter me from trying something that might improve my abilities. Some people say I'm gullible, since I love to try new ideas. I laugh with those who comment on my willingness to open my mind to so many thoughts; however, I know that, inside, I choose to try anything that my mind finds intriguing and with which I feel comfortable. I want to improve always in every area. Not everyone is driven (or gullible) in this way.

When I was at Stanford, a sports nutritionist asked me to keep a food journal. I love journaling, so this was an easy task. After a few weeks, we sat together to discuss my food habits. Her first concern was the late night habit of eating two to three bowls of Lucky Charms with nonfat milk. Lucky Charms seemed like eating sugary air, so did they really have a great impact on my afternoon performance?

Of course, down deep, I knew the answer to this question. But, I didn't have Lucky Charms growing up. I discovered those in college, and they were included with my scholarship. Changing this habit to a healthier choice benefitted not only my daily workouts but also my sleep and studies.

I heard what my nutritionist was saying, but I chose, for a while in my life, not to listen. When I personally realized that Lucky Charms didn't grant me the mental clarity I wanted and wasn't conducive to great sleep or great workouts the next day, I finally chose to stop eating them at night. The nutritionist's information wasn't bad; it was actually good. I just wasn't ready to listen or make a real change in food consumption.

No words will change anyone without action attached. Action is the only avenue for any real change. Personal conviction, study, and knowledge create a lasting change. Once I stopped eating non-fuel foods, my performance increased, my energy increased, I could focus on my studies better. I would fall asleep with my brain working on problems with skills or performance in the gym, and I would wake to ideas of how to solve those problems.

Throughout the years, I've become even more in tune with my body's ability to function based on the food I choose to ingest. A lot of diets tell you what to eat and what not to eat, foods to avoid and foods that your diet shouldn't be without.

I also recall when I was in college, one nutritionist focused on my fiber intake, while another insisted that I increase my protein amount. Recently, I came to the conclusion that most diets and decisions come down to answering this one question for me: *Do I feel light?*

This tool is so simple, which is usually the case when it comes to huge breakthroughs in personal change. This is the only question I need to ask myself. It makes my choice clear and quick.

Does that mean that I never eat foods that don't fit my criteria of being *Light*? No. But, I'm very aware when I do choose those kinds of foods, and I know beforehand how I should expect to feel as a result of that choice. I take full responsibility for those decisions.

I may choose the opposite of light if I don't need a sharp mind or high energy that day. However, it has become clear to me that when I want to receive inspiration, feel increased energy, make a difference, be in control of my emotions, or alleviate pain from my body, then I must choose light foods.

Light is synonymous with energy, clarity, direction, and agility. The opposite is true when we choose the absence of light, which makes us feel confused, dark, or lost, and physically heavy. We say phrases such as: "I feel full," "I feel stuffed," "I feel heavy," or "I feel tired."

If we think of food as a basis for our ability to function as an athlete, then words like *full, heavy, stuffed* and *tired* don't serve us well. Therefore, when choosing what to eat, you must first ask yourself, "What do I want?" or "How do I want to feel today?" (You can answer this in your morning GIFT journaling discussed in Chapter 2). Then be clear on why you want your goal.

Once you know what you want and why, then you've resolved the issues surrounding whether or not you're willing to sacrifice to get those results. In other words, what is the Range you're willing to live within in order to achieve your desired outcomes? After this crucial first step, you simply ask yourself this one question: **Do I feel LIGHT?**

Every choice you make with food will come from answering that question. What food to eat? How much food to eat? How often should you eat? If it makes you feel light by filling yourself with a light-based food, then you're telling yourself that this food will provide not only physical light, but also mental light and emotional light.

Think of your body as a new car. If you fill your car with the recommended high-octane fuel, then it will perform at its highest ability for you. In the same way, *give your body the good food that's perfect for it and it will give you high performance in the gym.*

This way of eating requires vigilant self-awareness. You're the only one who can decide what you should do. Becoming aware of how you feel in all areas of your life is hard work.

If someone challenged you to stop eating sugar, then you might choose to try that for a while. Most likely, you wouldn't continue to abstain from sugar forever because of someone else's words. You might be able to white-knuckle your way through the challenge for a few weeks.

However, if someone asked you how sugar made you feel, then you'd have to think about how your body feels after consuming sugar, decide what feelings are attached to those chemical reactions going on inside your body, and express your answer. It's much more time consuming initially. You must listen to what your body is telling you versus what the latest diet fad suggests is best for you.

Eventually, your body will quickly reject even the thought of eating certain foods. It will take time to overcome the habit of eating food to mask emotions that we don't want to confront, but in doing so, we gain a self-mastery over food and every part of our life that brings us into a presence with ourselves that's empowering. The food we choose will either increase or decrease our sensitivity to our own needs in life. We're all different, so you must come to your own conclusion to determine what your body is telling you.

The following is a simple food routine that I've used after years of being taught many philosophies and through deciding what works best for me personally:

My personal daily food choice:
1. Immediately after waking up, drink a large glass of water, and then drink plenty of water throughout the day.
2. Eat a balance of carbs to protein (approximately 200-300 calories) every 3 hours, including veggies & fruits (choose *Light* foods as much as possible).

3. Stop eating about 2-3 hours before bed.
4. Fast from all food and water 24 hours once or twice per month.

Every athletic trainer or specialist will repeatedly tell you to stay hydrated. This is crucial to performance and for everyday energy as well. Once my coach challenged our club team to never pass a water fountain without taking a sip.

This was inconvenient at times, but I tried to take on that challenge for years. Because of this habit, water is the first and last thing I fill my body with every day. I keep a water bottle with me everywhere I go. Thus, I no longer see a water fountain and hurry over to take a sip. Try to always have water on hand and sip throughout your day.

One theory says that eating six small meals per day will make us feel light, even if you eat Twinkies for every meal. The caloric intake may cause a weight loss, but the choice of food won't bring mental clarity in the same way that foods made from sunlight will. In my small meals (or feelings as many call them now), I simply ask myself, "Do I feel light?"

As I've said, this is the only gauge I choose to follow, and it works exceptionally well for me. Sometimes, my body doesn't want as much protein or carbs, so I just listen to my body and try to always include more light-based foods in my selection.

I also choose to do a 24-hour fast by abstaining from all food and drinks once or twice per month. I've included this practice since I was a beginning gymnast at a very young age. As an athlete, I always felt the benefits of this practice.

My energy levels were higher after a fast day. Recent research is showing a plethora of health benefits from fasting. Doctors currently encourage this practice of fasting for many people. When food is out of the picture for a little while, we're more sensitive to issues that may be beyond food for us. Fasting has been shown to increase energy. It's a natural body cleanser and it gives your body a sort of jump-start.

Food shouldn't always entertain us, although we often use food as entertainment and as a way of escaping emotions. We like to eat when we want to avoid confronting difficult issues in our lives. Food is often used as a buffer. We escape the reality of our lives by eating foods that keep us somewhat in a haze.

I used to be desensitized to what foods helped me perform optimally. I sometimes chose food as a social tool or a high emotional mask, but the older I get, the more sensitive I become to my daily functioning based on what I eat.

I continue to eat food for pleasure at times, but when I know I need to focus or want to create something great, or perform something impossible, then food is the first thing that's narrowed. My Cruise Control gets turned off and I keep my Range tight.

We all know the rule of the body game, which is, if you overeat, you'll be overweight. Being overweight as an athlete doesn't feel good. If you don't feel good, then you're at a higher risk for injury and you'll be more inclined to get emotionally upset or depressed. Don't let food be a barrier for your athletic career.

Food changes how you feel about yourself. How you feel about yourself changes what you choose to do during your day. What you choose during your day affects your workouts and ultimate life as a gymnast.

I don't like the idea of eating to "lose weight." There's a place for that, but, in general, I believe if you drink enough water and eat foods that lighten your body, you'll obtain the energy and mental clarity necessary to enjoy gymnastics at a level you intentionally want.

Eat food that increases your capacity to function and think clearly during practices. We all know when we choose unhealthy foods because of how we feel later. Our emotions, actions, and results are tied to how we treat our physical body. It's a very important part of changing our mental game.

Optimize your choices so you can optimize your athletic performance. Live within *The Range* that works best for you. Only you can decide that through trial and error, not by avoiding your real needs. Ask yourself, "Does this fill me with *LIGHT?*"

Everyone's body type is different. Most people believe a gymnast has "a look." From years of experience, I can tell you that there's no one-size-fits-all gymnast. Most people think it's best to be short if you're going to be a gymnast. The tallest gymnast on the Stanford women's gymnastics team when I was there was the only one to get a 10.0 on floor at a meet.

Many believe if you're not a level 10 by your sophomore year in high school, then you should just quit because you'll never get invited to a college team. Plenty of level-8 gymnasts become walk-ons and individualize in an event; some even receive scholarships.

If you worry about outside or external factors, then you're giving away your light and your power. Keep your body filled with light so it can be an instrument to help you fulfill your gymnastics dreams. Use *The Light Plan* to light your life with energy and power.

Chapter 3 Highlights

- Many food plans are provided by countless researchers, telling athletes what they should and shouldn't eat in order to become the highest level in their sport.

- After many years of being told what's best for me as an elite and collegiate athlete, I discovered my own personal plan, *The Light Plan*.

- This food plan is based on one question: Do I feel light?

- Every action stems from the answer to this question.

- Based on this question, you adjust the amount, timing, and choice of light foods until your workouts at gym are full of energy and emotional and mental strength.

- You monitor your own physical reactions to the types of foods you eat.

- Light foods include any food made by sunlight: vegetables, fruits, legumes, grains, nuts, dairy, and meat.

What's ahead in Chapter 4

Find out the quickest technique to calm your anxious body and mind at gym in seconds. Furthermore, when you struggle to relax at night after a long day of practice and other activities, use the tension-relaxation tool provided to put your mind and body to rest with ease.

Chapter 3 Action Items

Challenge:

1. Try to start your day intentionally increasing more water throughout your day. Eat foods that are created by light. Keep a record of how you feel as you increase the "light" foods throughout your days.
2. Keep a food journal until you find your own routine based on the question, "Do I feel light?"
3. Take time to be still after eating food and see what your body is telling you. You will begin to recognize a pattern of what foods

provide the energy required to accomplish your workouts optimally.

4

Calm

"The time to relax is when you don't
have time for it."

— Author unknown

"The main thing to do is to relax and
let your talent do the work."

— Charles Barkley

CHAPTER 4 TOOLS:

Two Relaxation Techniques

1. Tension-Relaxation:

Intentionally tighten muscles in a progressive order throughout your body in order to release tension, clear your mind, and feel the calm that comes from a fully relaxed physical state. Breathe out as you release your muscles, then keeping focused on your breathing rhythm as you prepare to move on to the next body part.

2. Quick Breathing:

Breathe in slowly for five seconds, hold your breath for five seconds, breath out and count down for five seconds. On the countdown, at the last second, say or think either "shoulders" as you drop your shoulders or your *Big Cue Word*.

Big Cue Word: A word you decide upon to remind you of *The Place,* which can be used during the *quick breathing technique.*

The Place: A calm, peaceful space you create mentally, where there are no obligations, concerns, or worries. It's a place just for you to enjoy during the *tension-relaxation* process.

When I was 15 years old, I was spending twenty to thirty hours per week in the gym. After workout, dinner, and studies, I would hurry to get to sleep. Normally, instead of sleeping, my mind would be reviewing skills and routines.

This increased my adrenaline, which wasn't conducive to sleep. Because of this, I used to have difficulty falling asleep. My dad taught me breathing techniques to help me let go of the gymnastics excitement that would typically keep me up at night.

The *quick breathing* tool specifically helped settle anxiety whenever I felt nervous about a particular skill during practice or right before I was about to perform at any competition. If I needed immediate emotional calmness and stress relief, I used the *quick breathing technique*. I focused on this tool to let go of emotions attached to intense situations within just a few seconds.

Unlike the *quick breathing tool*, however, the *tension-relaxation* is not a quick fix solution to stress. It is used as a nightly routine practice to allow every muscle a physical and chemical release from the daily excitement and adrenaline buildup.

Tension-relaxation includes breathing throughout the exercise, however, it takes more time and involves other components as well. This tool requires consistent daily time set aside for the greatest benefit.

It can also prepare your body for deep mental work which cannot be done in the 15 second *quick breathing technique*. Eventually, I added the *visualization* tool (refer to Chapter 5) that my brother taught me to my nighttime *tension-relaxation* routine.

Together, these methods helped me fall asleep, calm any anxiety during the day, and improved my overall abilities in the process.

Tension-Relaxation Technique
Begin any tension-relaxation routine with a comfortable sitting or lying position. Think about your breathing. Lie down with your hands on your stomach so you can feel your breathing pattern and your stomach rise and fall. Fill your chest, stomach, and diaphragm, sending oxygen to every part of your body. Once you fill your body with oxygen, and your mind is focused on your breathing rhythm, then begin a *tension-relaxation* practice.

The simplest form of this is to move either from head to toe, or toe to head. Take one part of your body, isolate and squeeze the muscles of just that part of your body as you breathe in, hold your breath and that tension, then relax and release those muscles and breathe out. Let the emotions leave your body and mind as you relax and breathe out the stress or high intensity that has built up throughout your day in that specific area of your body.

Focus on your breathing before going on to the next body part. Mentally tell yourself *breathe in, breathe out* in a calm, soothing manner.

Tighten the next part of your body once your breathing is regulated and restful. Repeat the process until you have tightened, released, and sent oxygen to every section of your body.

Start by tensing each muscle at 100%, or as tight and uncomfortable as you can. Think of sending all of your intense emotions, positive or negative, into the constricted muscle areas: up your leg, other leg, hands to upper arm, other arm, core, shoulders, upper back, neck, lower face, upper face, entire body.

Any stress, excitement, depression, and elation are funneling into those muscles as you breathe in. Hold that uncomfortable feeling and your breath for as long as you want. You then relax and release the emotions built up in the muscle as you breathe out. Feel the relaxation occur, as if you were floating in the ocean and the water is running over your weightless body.

This release of tension may also feel like you're sinking into the ground, or as if you have a handful of sand that seeps through your fingers in a relaxing manner. Use whatever helps you respond to the mental command of liberating your body from strain.

Continue this pattern of relaxation until you reach your shoulders. When you get to your shoulders, neck, and face area, do a series of descending intensity tension releases.

First, breathe in and gradually tense the shoulders at 100%, hold that pressure while funneling all conscious emotion into that area, then release the shoulder muscles, relax and breathe out. The muscles may feel weightless or heavy, sinking into the ground. Repeat the same shoulder muscle area tightening but at only 50% tension, and then again at 10%.

Move on to the neck and face areas as well. Feel the slight tension that builds up in those specific areas. Being aware of the increments helps increase the awareness during the day as well.

If you become aware of any tension build up during the day, you can use the *quick breathing technique* to help let those feelings go.

Tension relaxation is part of the preparation before you do any *visualization*. The process is simply tensing muscles while breathing in, making them uncomfortably tight, and focusing all thoughts on those muscles then feeling those same muscles discharge all tension, stress, and anxiety.

Be sure to breathe out as you release the muscles, then take a deep breath in to fill those same areas with new oxygen, breathe out, and move on to the next designated body part.

Feel your mind clear, your muscles relax, and your lungs fill with oxygen. For as many thousands of thoughts a person has daily, the mind can truly only focus on one thought at a time effectively. As your mind focuses on breathing and then tensing specific muscles, other distractions fall away. Your mind moves from the focus of emotions in certain muscle areas, then back to your breathing as you proceed throughout the tension-relaxation technique.

Once you have sufficiently relaxed all parts of your body, imagine yourself walking down stairs until you reach a door. You open the door to *The Place*. *The Place* is where you have absolute peace, secluded from the stress of the world. Your mind is still. *The Place* is just for you. There is nobody else there.

You decide whether you are wrapped in a blanket or sitting at a beach in a swimsuit, if you hear birds outside or the whisper of the wind through leaves in a tree, if you are sitting in a soft chair inside or basking in the sunlight, or if you smell home baked goods or the springtime flowers. This is a place your mind wants to go back to and remain.

Time stands still here. There are no obligations, no responsibilities, no worries, no stress, no guilt, and no fear. It's only you in *The Place*. Choose a word in this place that reminds you of how you feel or what you love about your place.

This word is what I call your *BIG Cue Word*. You can use this word throughout the day in the *quick breathing tool* (discussed next). Remain in this place as long as you want, then choose to go on to *visualization* (discussed in Chapter 5) for more intense work, or walk back out the door and up the stairs until you're focused just on your breathing again.

Many times, you'll fall asleep before you get to the stairs, or choose to stay in *The Place* until your mind relaxes enough to fall asleep. The relaxation tool prepares your mind to move on to visualization if you choose to go deeper and remain alert.

Quick Breathing Technique

During the day, I use a *quick breathing technique* with the *Big Cue Word* to help my mind remember *The Place*. It creates a chemical change in my body. I feel my shoulders drop, my heart rate slow, my mind clear, and my energy stabilize.

The *quick breathing* tool takes 15 seconds, and you can do this anywhere and anytime. Begin by focusing on your breathing. Breathe in for five seconds, hold your breath for five seconds, and then breathe out for five seconds, nice and slow. Sometimes, I choose to do this in 5-10-second increments.

Choose one targeted, yet inconspicuous muscle to tense as you breathe in and hold. As you breathe out slowly, counting 5, 4, 3, 2, 1, relax that muscle completely.

I incorporate a couple of other subtle additions to this technique. On the last count on the way down from the 15 second sequence, you can either say, outloud or in your mind, the word "shoulders" as you drop your shoulders or your *Big Cue Word* that you determined in *The Place* (discussed in the Tension Relaxation Tool).

For the last second of the countdown, instead of saying the number, tell yourself "shoulders" and drop your shoulders or the word you chose in *The Place*. Either word you use will have a valuable impact on your sense of peace.

Thus, there are two modifications of the basic *Quick Breathing technique* when counting down 5, 4, 3, 2, 1. One variation is 5, 4, 3, 2, *shoulders*, then drop your shoulders. The other variation is 5, 4, 3, 2, *Big Cue Word*. Only this last example takes your mind and body briefly, yet immediately to *The Place*.

Dropping your shoulders or using the *Big Cue Word* will create a chemical change inside your body. A calm washes over your entire body and you feel prepared to move forward once again.

Your mind is now refocused, your muscles are releasing tension, your breath is slowing the heart down, your thoughts are calm from the cue word, and you physically feel your shoulders drop. This short tool is incredibly effective and useful in any high-stress moment.

Once you are aware that your shoulders are rising, your eyebrows are furrowing, your breath is quickening, or your hands are sweating, then try using this technique to bring you back to a more stable mental, emotional, physical, and rational state. I often used this tool a few minutes before I would compete, when I felt moments of worry in practice, or at any time when I felt pressure.

The *Big Cue Word* creates an automatic chemical release, and your body responds. It's as if you just visited *The Place* in that one brief second of breath.

Breathing tools are easy exercises that allow you needed mental breaks. Your body responds when using a *Big Cue Word* to remind yourself of *The Place* when you don't have time to lie down for 30 minutes and go through the progressive steps.

The *Big Cue Word*, if applied correctly, will initiate positive physiological changes. Your heart rate will decrease, your breath will slow, your shoulders will drop, and your mind will relax. All these things will happen without having to mentally ask each area to do so. Your body will respond promptly to the *Big Cue Word.*

Chapter 4 Highlights

- Our bodies go through cycles of calm and stress during the day.

- As we become aware of the little physical changes that occur during increased tension, we can alleviate it quickly through the *tension-relaxation technique* or a *quick breathing technique.*

- *Tension Relaxation Technique* is a progressive routine of focusing on your breathing pattern while simultaneously tightening segments of your body, then releasing the muscles.

- This is a clear way to feel the difference between a relaxed versus a tense physical state.

- Both tools change your chemical physiological responses.

- The *Quick Breathing Technique* includes breathing in for five seconds, holding the breath for five seconds, then slowly breathing out for five seconds. Tighten one targeted, yet inconspicuous muscle on your in-breath and hold, then release the muscle slowly on your out-breath.

- Utilize the calming techniques to slow down your heightened, impatient, anxious and nonproductive self in order to feel, act, and think more clearly.

What's Ahead in Chapter 5

An added piece to this puzzle for greater relaxation is discussed more in detail in the next chapter. We will explore the powerful tool of ending your daily routine with visualization. Visualization will allow your mind to create meticulous images of who you want to become as if you already are that gymnast and perform those skills now.

Chapter 4 Action Items

Challenge:

1. Practice *Tension Relaxation* as you lie down at night.
2. Choose a *Big Cue Word* in *The Place* during the *Tension Relaxation* Technique to use during the day in the *Quick Breathing* Technique.
3. Be aware of the tension building up throughout the day and use the *Quick*

Breathing Technique to alleviate that tension and refocus your energy and mind.

5

Vision

"Some of the world's greatest feats
were accomplished by people not smart
enough to know they were impossible."
—Doug Larson

"Don't believe what your eyes are
telling you."
—Jonathan Livingston Seagull

"I close my eyes and I can see."
—Ziv Zaifman

CHAPTER 5 TOOLS

Visualization:

A mental practice used to create a result in the mind based on what you want the actual result to be outside of your mind in real life.

At the age of 16, my brother, David Neil, came home for the summer from college. David taught me not only how to swing dance but also an incredible life lesson of using positive affirmations and visualization to achieve great results. He knew I was an elite gymnast, but he also knew there was always so much more for me to work on.

David's enthusiasm for life and knowledge has always given me a desire for more wisdom as well. I chose to believe what he was teaching me regarding mental tools. I had a national team-qualifying meet coming up in Salt Lake City at the

Delta Center. At that time, there were three national teams: a developmental national team, a national team, and an international team. Two teammates and I were going to this meet with our coach, Lisa Spini, who recently coached Olympic alternate in Korea, Mykayla Skinner, from Desert Lights Gymnastics in Chandler, Arizona.

While David was home, about six months before this competition, he introduced me to the power of mind activities. He helped me write some affirmations in a manner that was very specific, and he helped me develop a night routine, which included visualizing a professional athlete perform my routines, then trying to see myself perform those routines. It was a crazy mess. My mind was out of control.

When I would visualize my body perform a triple full on floor, my mind would see a body twisting like helicopter propellers. A triple full is a tumbling pass that includes a backwards flip with a straight body rotating three times latitudinally before landing back on the ground.

The beam apparatus included constant falls and crashes. It was a slow process, which I continued only out of faith that David knew better than I did and so this would work for me. Eventually, I could see myself walking into the arena, wearing the competition leotard that my mom made for our team, and then performing in front of judges.

Details started to become clearer as my routines became mentally easier to see: how the leotard would feel, how the temperature would be, how many people might be in the audience. I had no true idea whether these things would or would not actually become reality because I had never stepped foot in the Delta Center prior to this meet.

My routines gradually got easier and easier in my mind, and, not surprisingly, they also became more consistent in the gym. I would visualize the one pass I was most concerned about on my floor routine more than any of the others. I came to know how my body responded to the ground, how my quadriceps and glutes would tighten on impact, how my chest would immediately lift confidently up, my arms reacting simultaneously to the stick, where my eyes would focus on the blue-carpeted floor first, then up to the crowd ahead of me.

It was exciting and consistent in my nightly routine. I woke to the affirmations, telling myself the words David had helped me create. Everything was as if my visions had already happened. And, on that fateful day, that's exactly how it did happen.

The Delta Center was similar to my imaginations. I wore the leotard my mind had seen, my hair was in the traditional tight ponytail, the routines had been completed as expected. I was on floor last at this particular competition. My triple full was decent for my standards. The pass coming up was the greatest concern I had had six months prior to this day. However, I felt no fear. I moved as if in a dream. I landed my second pass, a double tuck. When I landed, my body responded, my quads and glutes reacted, my chest lifted, my eyes focused, my arms flew up to position to create the perfect double tuck for me.

In that brief moment, I found my mind wondering, "Am in bed at home, or am I at the Delta Center?" It was an out-of-body experience, one that I've re-lived in my mind many times since. The power of the mind was sold to me in that instant. I knew I would never be the same. And I wasn't.

If you believe that you cannot change or be successful, then you'll most likely have that be your reality. If you're not moving forward, then you're essentially living in a dreamlike state or living as a past version of yourself. This past version of you becomes your constant present. Thus, you're choosing to live in the past presently.

If you want to live in the past, change nothing. If you have a desire to make a change, then there is a sense of belief in your thoughts that is currently happening. The feelings associated with these beliefs are chemical vibrations inside you. These vibrations are recognized as hopefulness, gratitude, and energy.

Visualization is one of the most powerful tools available for athletes. Since that pivotal moment in my life, I've worked with sports psychologists who have reiterated the same visualization technique. My routine included positive affirmations in the morning, cue words during workouts (words to focus my mind), then tension-relaxation and visualization to fall asleep at night. When working with visualization, you need to be patient and realize it takes extensive practice to build the skill. This is just like building a muscle, and it takes consistent practice.

A simple way to practice visualizing is by holding an orange and memorizing every detail of it.

Then, close your eyes and work with the orange in your mind. Using all your senses, try to look at the orange, smell the orange, and finally taste the orange, all within your mind.

What does the orange look like? Is it a dark orange or a light orange? Does it have lots of bumps or thick skin? Is it easy to peel in one try, or does it require many little peels? Does it have seeds and lots of juice? Can you see the orange spray as you peel the orange?

Use as many senses as you can in order to better prepare for the actual changes you desire to make in your mind through visualization practice. The orange drill will prepare you to go into deeper visualization levels.

Visualization has three common perspectives.

Visualization Perspectives

1. External professional:

You visualize a professional person performing or engaged in the activity of your choice in a perfect or ideal manner, as if you're in the audience watching that person.

2. External personal:

You are visualizing yourself performing exactly as the professional did, as if you're in the audience watching yourself perform perfectly.

3. Internal personal:

You're visualizing everything about the performance personally. You're engaged in the experience directly.

Perspective #1 is the *external professional*. Do some research and find a professional athlete who you aspire to become like. Find someone who's similar in body type, style, and easy to feel a connection to. Get to know this professional and how they move, perform, and the confidence they exude. Observe and focus on how the professional responds to the floor or the vault.

Find video footage of the professional doing the exact same skills that you're currently working to perfect. Use the video of that skill and watch it over and over. Try to feel the rhythm and the reactions that the professional is experiencing. Then, close your eyes and watch the professional perform that skill in your mind, just like you watched on the video.

Picking the perfect role model for you requires awareness. We may glorify someone in one area and want to be just like that person. The person you admire may seem to have it all together; however, most likely, there may be areas in their life that you would choose not to emulate. Pick the skill you're working on in your life; choose the perfect role model for you to study and use in Perspective One, the *external professional perspective*. Then move to the next skill and that role model may change to be someone new.

Perspective #2 is the *external personal perspective.* Once you can clearly see every move of a professional athlete performing your skill to your desired satisfaction, then work on seeing yourself from a distance. It's as if you're watching yourself on a video or in the audience. Practice closing your eyes and see yourself perform the skill with ease and perfection. When you're unable to see it perfectly, then immediately replace yourself with the professional again. Don't allow yourself to see less than perfect performances. Get comfortable watching your body replace the professional body's rhythm and swing, style, and confidence. You'll find your own personality come through when your mind feels consistent in understanding how you want your body to maneuver through each skill.

Perspective #3 is the most difficult and, accordingly, the most powerful perspective step in visualization. It's called the *internal personal perspective.* When you're able to consistently close your eyes, feel yourself perform the specific skill perfectly and every other sensation that goes with that moment, then your body responds appropriately. It's a deja vu experience.

You'll feel the floor beneath your feet, the tightness of the leotard and your hair pulled up, the positioning of a coach on the side of floor, the color of carpet, the energy bubbling up as the excitement to perform and anticipation builds, the beating of your heart, the determination in your eyes, and the stuck skills that follow.

Your mind is powerful and memorizes what you want to have happen. Whatever you allow yourself to see, hear, feel, think and believe is that to which your body will respond. Any result in your life is just a projection of your thoughts and feelings.

Nothing can compare to this feeling of performing a perfect skill that you've mastered to your best ability after all the physical and mental work you've done to create this moment. When you don't know if you're at home in bed seeing this skill in your mind or actually at the gym performing the skill, then you know you've mastered something great. It feels exactly the same.

I still consider myself a gymnast. I only have to close my eyes to get the exact feeling that I used to experience when I was tumbling across the blue floor at the AZ Twisters Gymnastics facility in Mesa, Arizona. Roe Kruetzer, the Arizona Twisters gym owner, would walk around, clapping to the beat of our floor routine music and sprinkling fairy dust to make us fly during our beam routines. Lisa Spini, would do spontaneous intersquad meets, or teach us technical dance skills on Fridays. It all comes back so clearly because I vividly watched every aspect of my workouts or my performances in my mind before falling asleep at night.

Before you begin any visualization practice, you must have decided what you want. This is the answer to the question that was presented in the Introduction and is a recurring theme throughout this book: Cruise Control--The Range. Be sure to already have written what you want and why you want it. Once this is in place, then you'll be practicing visualization as a bedtime ritual.

At night, after you've completed the tension-relaxation tool, go through a visualization routine. Visualize in the three different perspectives, remembering to default to Perspective One if Perspective Two or Three isn't working out well. Don't worry if this takes longer than you'd like it to. You might find that you stay with Perspective One most of the time. Visualize what you want to have happen as if you already experienced it and are just reliving the experience.

Be as detailed as possible. See the environment, feel the temperature, smell the air, look at your attire, observe what others are doing around you, then continue toward the actual event. The event may be a specific skill you're working to perfect, or a competition coming up in six months.

The situation can be anything you want to review and obtain mental control over, before you actually perform. It can be a specific skill, routine, competition, relationship with a coach or teammate, or an overall feeling about gymnastics. Always visualize the event from a place of predetermined emotions. Do you want to feel excited, calm, confident, humble, inspired, or capable?

Walk yourself into the experience by beginning with a breathing focus, and then back out with a refocus on your breathing. This process takes time and must be used consistently to realize any significant outcome. Our thoughts are the only thing that we can truly change. Visualization is the catalyst that jump-starts a lasting change for our present and future.

Visualize yourself as a
Flippin' Awesome Gymnast!

Chapter 5 Highlights

- The visualization tool is part of your night routine as you're preparing to fall asleep.

- Once you've completed the tension-relaxation technique, your mind is ready to watch yourself become and perform what you aspire to be.

- You will visualize through three different perspectives: professional external, personal external, and personal internal.

- All three perspectives require vigilance and hard work to reap the benefits.

- It takes time to develop the mental muscles necessary to see in the mind's eye what you want your body and environment to conceive.

- Put visualization into regular practice and you just might find that you're actually living your dream.

What's ahead in Chapter Worksheets

As you implement the chapter tools incorporated into these worksheets, you'll generate a daily plan to increase your efficiency, energy, focus, and drive. You'll also see your own personal athletic success clearly in your mind. Your goals will be defined and almost tangible. You'll see how to take the methods discussed and put them into action by completing the worksheets provided.

Chapter 5 Action Items

Challenge:

1. Decide on a professional or high-level gymnast who executes skills that you want to improve upon in gym. Study and observe how this role model responds to situations and performs each movement of those desired skills.

2. Use this professional example in perspective one of your visualization tool.

3. Try using all three perspectives of visualization after you've finished your tension-relaxation breathing technique before bed for two weeks.

4. Write in your journal any changes you've noticed in your own skill development from experimenting with this technique.

APPENDIX I

CHAPTER WORKSHEETS

Chapter 1: No Cruise Control

Ponder and Write in your Journal:

Find Your Range:

1. Who are you, outside of being "a gymnast"?

2. Why do you do gymnastics?

3. What do you want from gymnastics?

_____

_____

_____

4. Why do you want that?

_____

_____

_____

5. What are the obstacles in the way of achieving your goal?

_____

_____

_____

6. Change the word *obstacles* to *opportunities* from question #5.

_____

_____

_____

7. What are you specifically willing to do to get there?

_____

_____

_____

Chapter 2: GIFT

Challenge: Write in a morning and evening journal for 30 days.

Morning Journal Writing, The GIFT:
G = Gratitude, write one to five things you're grateful for about being a gymnast

_____

_____

_____

I = Inspiration, after reading, "free-write" your thoughts about gymnastics

_____

_____

_____

F = Feeling, write the answer to the questions: "How do I want to feel today?" "What will I do to make that happen?"

_____

_____

_____

T= Thoughtfulness, write down one or two names of people you'll serve today at gym.

_____

_____

_____

Evening Journal Writing, Review:
Be accountable to yourself, your goals, your morning action plan in the GIFT. Write what happened and how you'll change something tomorrow to get closer to your desired outcome.

_____

_____

_____

Chapter 3: LIGHT

Challenge:

1. Today, I drank _____ounces of water.

2. Before I ate food today, I asked myself, "Will this fill me with light?"

3. Daily Food Journal:

　　Date:　Food:　Amount:　Time:　Feel:

_____

_____

_____

_____

_____

_____

_____

_____

4. Keep a daily food journal until you are aware of how your food choices make you feel.

_____

_____

_____

_____

5. This month I fasted, drinking no liquids and eating no food for 24 hours.

During the fast, I felt:

_____

_____

_____

_____

_____

_____

_____

After the fast, I felt:

_____

_____

_____

_____

_____

_____

Chapter 4: CALM

Journal:

1. Today I used the quick breathing technique when:

_____

_____

_____

_____

_____

_____

2. Using the Tension-Relaxation technique at night helps me

_____

_____

_____

_____

_____

_____

Chapter 5: VISION

Journal:

1. The change I am making in my life is:

_____

_____

_____

2. My role model is:

_____

_____

_____

3. Last night, during visualization, I used Perspective ___(1, 2, and/or 3).

_____

_____

_____

4. Using this perspective made me feel:

_____

_____

_____

_____

_____

_____

_____

_____

_____

_____

_____

APPENDIX II

STRONG MIND WORKSHEET

1. Try this new daily routine for 30 days, record your commitment level, your planned versus actual results, and how you feel throughout this activity.

  a. Morning:

      Drink a large glass of water and throughout the day

      Take off Cruise Control as you choose your Range during your Morning GIFT.

- **Gratitude** (write one to five things you're grateful for):

      _____

      _____

      _____

      _____

      _____

- **Inspiration** (write what sparks your fire of excitement to go to gym today, review your goals for gymnastics, read your two affirmations ten times daily. Say it, see it, feel it, believe it as if it has already happened.

_____

_____

_____

_____

_____

- **Feeling** (How do you want to feel at gym today? What will YOU do and choose to think in order to feel that?):

_____

_____

_____

_____

_____

- **Thoughtfulness** (Who can you be kind to and help at gym today? Write one or two names):

_____

_____

_____

_____

b. Day:

Choose the LIGHT Plan

- Ask yourself, "Do I feel light?" Then choose foods that increase your energy at gym. Keep a log of the foods you eat, and look for patterns with your energy levels.
- Surround yourself with positive energy and people.
- Create your cue words for every move in your gymnastics routines
- Keep your Mind Guard up, only let positive thoughts enter your mind.

c. Night:

- Take responsibility for your day in a quick night journal.
- What did you like/ not like about gym today?
- How will you make your workout better tomorrow?
- Enjoy tension-relaxation as you lie down at night.
- Visualize:
- Use the three different perspectives

CONGRATULATIONS AND THANK YOU
FOR READING THIS BOOK AND
WORKING TO CREATE YOUR PERSONAL
ELITE-LEVEL DAILY ROUTINE!

About the Author

#1 Best Selling Author Amy Twiggs is a wife and a mother of four teenagers. She is a former elite gymnast and, in 1993, she was a member of the developmental National Women's Gymnastics Team. She received a full-ride athletic scholarship for gymnastics from Stanford University where she obtained a Bachelor's Degree in Psychology with a focus in Health & Development. Mental Training is her passion. Amy's education has provided many opportunities for her to give back to athletes. She has coached and choreographed for 25 years at a variety of gymnastics facilities. She is a former USAG Judge and currently owns the Flippin' Awesome Gymnastics facility in St. George, Utah.

If you are interested in contacting Amy Twiggs please email her at

flippinawesomecoaching@gmail.com